Freedom to Achieve

How 'One Team' Took Forest Holidays from Ordinary to Extraordinary

By Gary Fletcher

CEO Forest Holidays

2006-2014

Copyright © 2014 Gary Fletcher
All rights reserved.
ISBN-10: 1503259471
ISBN-13: 978-1503259478

Here's What's Inside...

4   **Introduction**

6   **Our Humble Beginning...**

9   **How Our Team Took the Business to Another Level...**

15 **Why Good Isn't Good Enough...**

22 **The Magic Behind Our Business...**

26 **How Our Culture Sets Us Apart...**

35 **The Proof Is in the Pudding...**

37 **Why the Future Looks Bright...**

40 **Here's How to Learn More about Forest Holidays...**

42 **About The Author...**

44 **A Massive Thanks...**

Introduction

Freedom to Achieve!

December 2014
Derbyshire, UK

When I look back at where Forest Holidays' started, I can't help but be impressed by how far we've come and the obstacles we've had to overcome to get there. The Forest Holidays team has taken an ordinary company and turned it around into something extraordinary and profitable. They've turned our company into something really magical and I wanted to capture how that came to be. I hear what a great company we have from all angles of the business; from our shareholders, customers, from our suppliers and directly from our team members.

I wanted to capture the success story we've become for three reasons; first, to understand and record business success. It's important to now and again stop and look back at where we've come from. The numbers don't lie.

Second, I wanted to recognize the fantastic team that has delivered the vision. It hasn't always been easy. We've had some really challenging times along the way. For instance, in the midst of the worst financial climate in the history of the world, we had to raise an enormous amount of money, in a short amount of time. Raising this much capital was really really difficult and we almost didn't make it several times, but it's the people on our team who went that extra mile that made the difference and made us the success story we are today.

Third, I want to remind the team to keep our culture as the business grows. It seems as companies get more and more successful, they often lose what made them such a success in the beginning. If I can capture that here today, it may help pave the way for where the company is heading next.

This book is a salute to each and every one of the team members, past and present, who have helped shape the company into what it is today. Without them, this story could have been very different!

To Our Continued Success!

Gary Fletcher

Our Humble Beginning...

The Forest Holidays we know today didn't start out that way. The Forestry commission is a brilliant organisation that manages Britain's Forests and had developed a small holiday cabin business some decades earlier. They had the tremendous foresight to recognise it needed a respected joint venture partner now with capital & commercial focus to allow the business to grow further.

Worldwide interest in the tender process was understandable, although it took over 18 months which everyone agreed did not help the business and when we arrived at the doorstep in 2006, the business was in decline, it was losing money and the occupancy was very low. In fact, the campsite occupancy was higher than the cabins, which is incredible seeing as one was inside and one was outside in a difficult UK climate. That's the reality of where we started. What we did have though was a fantastic brand and some beautiful sites in stunning locations and together with the Forestry Commission we set about improving the business.

The team had low morale because the business was in decline with customers complaining, head office was not able to support correctly and there was a distrust between the staff. We essentially had to start over and had to redesign the company, the product and the people and piece it all together.

To further illustrate where we started, let's not forget:

- The business was in decline and with full accounting practices turned just over £1m and was loss making.

- As the business was in effect 18 months in 'sale mode' most of the Support Centre team had left. The team members that remained were either temporary, on maternity or on long term sickness.

- When Forest Holidays was relocated to the Midlands from Edinburgh in 2006, only 1 part time Reservations Agent, came with the business. Morale was low and belief in the business was non-existent.

- All site managers were self-employed. They had a lot of self interest and were strangely incentivised by having no customers turn up. The measurements by which they were managed were not complimentary to a growing business; the more customers who came, the less they received in bonus?

- The IT platform was about to be turned off by the IT Company as it was so antiquated it could no longer be supported. The process for booking online was to make a booking and wait to receive a call back (when reservations agents had processed it) to confirm a booking or not.

- Cabins were aimed at the top of the market, but were not fit for the customer segment; school style dormitories, bench seating, poor fittings, sparse and uncomfortable furnishings, poor quality kitchens, orientation of sofas and seats was towards the TV and wall rather than the floor to ceiling glass – engaging with the forest flora and fauna and wildlife – the magical forest.

- In fact, when the new Forest Holidays took over there was only 1 style of cabin, which quickly moved to standard, superior and VIP. When the team suggested VVIP; which is clearly ridiculous; the categories moved to where they are today of Copper Beech, Silver Birch and Golden Oak.

- The cabins were aimed at upmarket customers who valued the British countryside and forests; very often able to entertain themselves, and did not want or need central entertainment facilities. It became clear quickly that the forest was the entertainment itself and that this was to be a very cabin centric product.

How Our Team Took the Business to Another Level...

We had to completely transform the company to turn it into what it is today. We started with the raw ingredient, which fortunately was that all these sites were in stunning locations; absolutely top drawer. These were all built in forests or surrounded by forests overlooking water. Furthermore we had a respected and strong Forestry Commission organisation behind us and with their Director Dr Bob Macintosh on the board it felt like a fresh start for the company. (The Forestry Commission have been and continue to be invaluable support and help for the business as it has matured over the years)

I was convinced with the above 2 ingredients we could turn what we had into something quite special, a brand of many sites, something different that was not available in the UK at the time.

At the time it was common for families to be split up on a typical UK holiday site; dad goes in the bar, mom goes for a treatment and the kids do activities, so they all do their own thing.. Holiday sites had several hundred accommodation units with lots of indoor central and social facilities for bad weather.

We wanted to put something together different; a genuine experience, one where the entertainment is the forest with small number of cabins with great personal service.

Everyone told us this wouldn't work, but we held our ground and went with our instinct.

We spent quite a lot of time differentiating ourselves from the competition. Our cabins are further away from anyone else so you have privacy; feeling like you have your own piece of the forest. The specification of each cabin is really high quality; there are no central facilities so you don't have to contend with lots of people, loud music and an urban atmosphere.

What we offer, that's different, is peace and quiet, tranquility, get away from it all. One of the real drivers is that we're all busy people in the UK, crammed in a small place, so we're all driving around or sitting in queues, with lots of stress. One of the key trends in UK holidays is spending quality time with each other when you have time off. We wanted to create a short break destination to recharge the batteries with their partner, with their children, together.

So exactly how did we develop the company to where it is today? Every time we had our backs up against the wall, it was the skill, focus and determination of the individuals and team that pulled us through. Every time, they delivered the answer and moved the business to the next level. Every person has played a critical part in this small company; each individual doing that bit extra and pulling in the same direction is what got us to where we are today.

One of the reasons the individuals and teams gave so much inside and outside of working hours, is because they felt like part of the business (as if it's their own), they feel valued and they enjoy the challenge we faced. Having trust, being empowered and given the freedom to achieve are some of the key ingredients for our success. When we talk about the Forest Holidays team members this not only includes the directly employed team, but a vast array of people connected with the business; banks, solicitors, suppliers – building and operational, consultants, advisors, financiers, investors, all of these played critical roles in the success of the business.

Trust, freedom to achieve and empowerment are the foundation of Forest Holidays' success. As the business develops and gets bigger, the core values will be hard to maintain, although important if Forest Holidays is to continue to outperform the market in every detail.

When asked why I think Forest Holidays is successful, I point out our values and vision and how we align people. Richard Whitwell, a key figure through the years in the business (Finance Director 2006-2009, Board member & fundraiser) agrees and adds a commercial perspective and says it comes down to a few commercial principals which we applied which he believes were cornerstones to why we are successful:

- (a) matching brand position with growing market trends
- (b) developing a cabin product that supports the market trends
- (c) trusting our instincts rather than expensive corporate advisors

To that last point, here's what a few of the so called experts told us when we were starting out:

> *'You will never develop an all-year- round business in the UK without considerable indoor facilities'.*
>
> *'The business model you are aiming for is fundamentally unsustainable with so few cabins per site and very little secondary spend!'*

Rather than discourage us, this criticism pushed us even more. To pull off the turn-around we needed a multi-skilled and highly motivated team, to build high quality cabins at unbelievable value for the money.

By far the most important step in forming a new company was to get leaders together early on and set out putting down the vision and values of the company – what are we going to do and how are we going to go about it?

Our Vision and Values

When you have a company it is critical to understand and develop why you are there, what are your goals and focus and what values are you going to live by? Recruit and manage your team in line with your vision and values and treat your customers with the same values. It's a challenge to sometimes balance commercial resources with values, but in the end that is what sets you apart from others, holding true to your values.

Vision:

To be the most recommended holiday provider in the UK. (I think we are there! – see net promoter score on page 14)

Values:

Genuine
Being genuine is our approach to all aspects of our work, our suppliers and each other. We genuinely care about the experiences our customers have on our sites. We have a real and honest concern about the forest and a responsibility towards it. Above all, we genuinely believe in Forest Holidays and are ambassadors for the brand at all times.

Commercial
Commerciality is at the core of all we do. Each of us makes decisions as if the business is our very own. Weighing up the options, consulting with others as needed, then making decisions based on facts and judgement. We recognise also that investment may be needed in order to create the right return.

One Team
We are one team regardless of job, role or location – and teamwork brings the best results; sharing experiences, discussing solutions, working across teams, to deliver against agreed actions. We take an interest in our colleagues around us and their well-being and work together to make the workplace a better place to be.

Passionate
Passion for our brand is what energises us. We feel privileged to be part of the Forest Holidays team and have a real drive to see as many customers as possible benefiting from the unique Forest Holidays experience. Our passion is contagious and motivates those around us.

Focused
With objectives set, we focus on successful delivery, however tough the challenges or distracting the diversions. Problem solving, negotiating positive outcomes, attention to detail and clear communication to those around us, are at the heart of our success. We remain set on winning and achieving.

Why Good Isn't Good Enough....

In the UK, service is not brilliant when compared to the US and other countries around the world. We haven't got a great reputation for our service as a whole. When companies provide great service, it really stands out, because it's amongst many that don't. Great service is a real passion of mine and quite early on I engaged an organization called Results International, and John Brown to help us improve our service levels greatly.

Because just providing good service is not good enough, it's got to be outstanding service so people will recommend you. And in the end, that's probably the easiest way to grow. We needed to make sure our service is exactly where it should be. Because we're small, we can be personal and engage the customer much better because we've only got around 60 cabins on each site, another differentiator for us.

Extraordinary Matching Shoes is the name Forest Holidays uses to catch the phrase "outstanding customer service". It is a golden thread which runs throughout the company and embodies an attitude, culture and spirit to do the best possible for our customers. It's a catchy way of explaining customer service.

In order to take our game to a higher level, we had to appreciate the massive difference between standard customer service which produces customer satisfaction and extraordinary customer care that creates customer pleasure and delight.

The three elements that make up our unique customer model that was designed just for Forest Holidays, integrates three simple ideas that are easy to implement on a consistent basis, providing **EXTRAORDINARY** service by **MATCHING** our customer's needs through putting ourselves in their **SHOES**.

Using EMS has no boundaries and we encourage each other to always think about it in everything we do and every interaction we have. The great thing about EMS is that it gives us a mechanism to pull together all the pieces of our 'success jigsaw'. It is a way to demonstrate our values, not just talk about them, and a lever to bring our Vision from a statement or purpose to a matter of fact.

EXTRAORDINARY
There's a catch in the word extraordinary. Overtime the word has tended to mean something amazing that tends to happen occasionally, or as a 'one-off'.

The way to do extraordinary is to consider the ordinary in a situation and then add something more to it; a bit like adding a few grains of salt to a soup.

It doesn't take much to enhance the flavour and the difference can make a real difference.

The difference that makes a difference...

What is an example of being extraordinary? It can range from the initial warm positive welcome to customers to other aspects of their stay. The way people are welcomed often colours the customer's thinking for the rest of their stay with us. Are we welcomed in a fairly standard expected way, or was the welcome genuine, making us feel special and glad we chose Forest Holidays?

We have a process for the team called 'speed stuns'- when a guest mentions something not working or an issue of any nature – they write it down in their EMS Speed stuns notebook and inform the guest when it will be dealt with i.e. 3 pm later that afternoon. Then they organise themselves into a team and ensure it is done earlier i.e. 12 noon; a system and process for under-promising and over-delivering.

Another example of how this shows up is our romantic 1 bed hideaways. We have some special little gifts for guests that they do not expect - from 'love heart sweets', marshmallow kits for 2, special bubble bath/toiletries for the large 2 person bath, and flowers & champagne. None of these are expected, so when they are received they feel special and personalized.

Every guest gets a rubber duck with our logo on to let them know the hot tub has been checked by the cleaning team. It sits on top of the hot tub when the inspection has been carried out.

All guests have a scrabble set and the FH team sets up the letters to say 'welcome Mr. & Mrs. ....' Just another way we show we are glad they are here with us. Very often the guests leave a note in scrabble letters on the board in return; "Thanks for great holiday", "Best holiday ever", "We will be back", etc., etc.

It's also worth mentioning that extraordinary doesn't mean over the top – which can be as bad as a poor welcome.

MATCHING
Matching is the component of EMS that can be quite easy to miss or overlook, yet when you put it into the formula, it can make a visible and tangible difference almost immediately. The effect of good matching will mean creating an instant connection with the customer. They will like you, and with that, they will like the brand too.

The way you achieve this, is by observing someone's look and returning it. Consider matching someone's tone, volume and speed without copying or imitating them. Look and be interested in what they find interesting. Talk about what they want to talk about.

Matching is probably the part of the EMS that requires the most practice, yet it is fun and helps our team to become excellent communicators in the long term. Like Extraordinary, there's nothing difficult about Matching and with some practice it simply becomes part of how we consistently deliver excellent customer care.

SHOES
The idea of 'walking in someone else's shoes' has been around for a very long time. It's all about rapport and the word Shoes in EMS is about putting yourself in the customer's Shoes as often as possible in order to really understand what they most need and what actions are required to satisfy this need. When you mentally 'wear' the Shoes of your customer in a genuine manner, what you're now

aware of is very significant. In fact you suddenly realise what steps you need to take to truly service the customer.

As a result of the outstanding service we provide our scores, which are independently reported by Customer Service Network, rank us in the top 10% of companies in the world. This is a testament to how our EMS is not just lip service. We live and breathe this philosophy at every level of the company.

EMS Champions

As Forest Holidays grows, more sites are developed and the team has grown considerably from a handful at the start of 2006 to several hundred. How do you keep this strong, positive culture as the business develops?

The answer according to Richard Jee, Forest Holidays Operations Director was to develop a national role of EMS Champion based at the Support Centre and one Champion on every site. The role of the National and Site EMS Champions is:

- Keep Forest Holidays culture alive and vibrant in each location.
- Recruit service orientated and quality people with the right attitude.
- Establish training modules so anyone in the company can progress if they choose.
- Regularly review performance and manage accordingly.

Examples of EMS Award Winning Actions:
Site teams are in position to solve customer challenges, do what it takes to give customers a great holiday – DELIVERY OF EMS.

Heroic actions in Yorkshire:

In Yorkshire, Rob Mackie at Keldy cabin site, helped to reunite a family with their dad who had gotten lost on the moors on a bike ride from our site on a day of severe gales. The agencies were sending out warning signals not to go outdoors, yet this family went out on a bike ride and the dad had got lost in this gale and the local emergency services wouldn't go out because it was so dangerous. Unbeknownst to us, Rob Mackie went out on his own with the wife of the family and found the man and brought him back to his poor children. We would not have advocated that if we'd known because of how dangerous it was.

It shows the commitment to the customer beyond anything that we would have asked of our team members. But he wanted to, he's a good person, he's got the right attitude, he wants to resolve the situation. That's the sort of loyalty we are talking about here. When you give team members the right environment, they reward you with their loyalty way above and beyond what you would ask.

Flew back from Europe for 1 customer:
Richard Harris, a support crew team member at Forest Of Dean, had been training as a relief Ranger. On one occasion he came back early from holiday in order to cover an activity that otherwise would have been cancelled and resulted in disappointed guests as well as lost revenue. With several positive comments on trip advisor for his Ranger sessions his overall can do attitude means that he is always focused on Extraordinary Matching Shoes.

The Shirt Off Their Backs:
One of our guests flew in to Glasgow and lost their suitcase; one of the team members, again unbeknownst to us, lent them clothes for their stay; loaned them their own clothes to make sure that they weren't disadvantaged with their holiday. A husband and wife team brought them over clothes. Now, they may have had to buy one or two bits as well but that's an example of someone going above and beyond. You don't see the airlines doing that do you?

Note:
EMS Champions are the right people to develop the culture of Forest Holidays, not Human Resources people. Helen Bacon is the appointed National EMS champion and has held various positions with the company since the business started, a great team player to help drive our service delivery & retain our positive culture.

The Magic Behind Our Business...

The magic to an outstanding service orientated company is not one thing, but a combination of several, all interlinked together which spells what is often referred to as a 'culture'.

> **Culture** - *the way of life, especially the general customs and beliefs, of a particular group of people at a particular time.*

Forest Holidays' culture is many things; the site teams, the Support Centre, the Directors, the Board, the Forestry Commission; build team, companies that supply the business it's a combination of all of these things, but what it stands for is a great company.

Examples of Culture at work in Forest Holidays:

> **Trust** - Forest Holidays does not have to make its Support Centre and National team members 'clock in' at set times. In fact the Support Centre hours are 8.30-5pm with 30 minutes lunch. But no one really pays much attention. It is about getting the results.

What does this mean?

Let's take the timekeeping example; not staying long hours to show you are working hard; many people in companies are at work but not really delivering much??

Forest Holidays people are results focused and time is scarce, so if it's more efficient to be at home to get the results, then that's OK, whatever it takes to get the job done. If you need to be in Scotland at 4.30am so be it. This is the freedom to achieve and be responsible for your own time to get the required results.

'Output' focused not 'input'. This means that when clear objectives are set with regular review meetings the team member is not micromanaged on how to achieve; or constrained by time. Results and the output is measured, not how they got there.

Senior Management is encouraged to build 'thinking time' into their schedule whether it is in a gym, at McDonalds or a local hotel, whatever works. But "spend plenty of time sharpening the saw" before you cut the tree down. Many people call this 'working on the business – not in it'.

Over the years some team members struggle with "Freedom to achieve"; as you are fully accountable and responsible for your own results. I would go as far as to say you have to have courage to back yourself; particularly in the early days of the business.

Very few team members have abused this freedom and if they do are managed out of the business as they stand out very strongly. This is often a 2-way mistake; Forest Holidays has recruited incorrectly and the individual is not delivering results.

Team

Forest Holidays is proud of its team culture; and that means the widest possible team; from internal to external people and companies (suppliers and contractors). The companies and individuals working with the company often talk about how they like working with the company, feel valued and share risks.

There are hundreds of examples of different departments helping each other out in challenging times; often with no benefit for themselves. Nowhere is this more evident than in new site openings with tight deadlines. There are hundreds of little details that need to be addressed and all hands on deck is often seen; from Contractors working through the night, to support centre people helping out over weekends and doing all kinds of work and the new on site team straining everything to hit deadlines. (We have of course given ourselves no room for error as the site opening date was set and bookings taken some 40 weeks beforehand; when first digger hit the soil!).

One of the great practices on new sites is to have soft launches where our 'wider team' and particularly the build team and contractors have their families to stay the weekend before paying guests. This team are really proud of their work and rightly so and it shows their families where they have been for last 40 weeks? This process also ensures everything is working correctly for our customers.

Can Do Attitude

This is a strong trait running through the company and again there are so many obstacles that get in the way of a growing business and team. Every time an obstacle is encountered a new route is found;

obstacles brushed aside through creativity, innovation and just absolute determination to succeed and never give up.

A couple of big challenges the team have faced:

First big challenge was the business plan authored in 2005/6 did not survive the first year of operation; selling pre manufactured lodges was a main strategy and it was clear this was not going to work for so many reasons and so the model changed from sales to rental only and from buying lodges off the shelf to manufacturing our own designed cabins and erecting on site. This transformation occurred within 6 months.

Another is when the main contractor on first large site development went into administration at the same time as the business was fund raising? After much soul searching the situation turned around to the businesses massive advantage in both short and long term. The best people from the main contractor were taken into the business and an in house build team developed using the best and known sub contractors, whom most have stayed with Forest Holidays throughout.

There are many smaller operational obstacles encountered such as using microwave dishes to provide IT connectivity in remote forest locations, using clever green technologies to heat cabins and hot tubs , delivering goods to cabins even in snow using on site tractors, etc.

How Our Culture Sets Us Apart...

Most companies have an average culture, and the people are often pulling in different directions which can cause huge inefficiencies and wasted time and effort for the progressive business. To get all the team focussed and pulling in same direction (Vectorship) is a challenge.. The Forest Holidays Team output is a truly vectored effort, all pulling in the same direction; performing and working more than most; doing outstanding things in and for the business, and themselves because they want to and want to be part of this great, growing business success.

Nowhere better is this demonstrated than in the build team at Forest Holidays; An eclectic team from varied backgrounds and skill sets but all equally focussed on 'Building Holidays not Houses'.

Ron & Aaron Brown & Mike with their brilliant construction and building skills, mixed with project , design & cost managers (John Allen, Andy Brook & Chris Brooks) creates a healthy tension that defines the fantastic cabin sites. This marshalled by Rich Palmer and Dan Parish to build quality partnerships & relationships with suppliers and contractors; (architects, plumbers, timber frame manufacturers, ground workers etc) to build 'one team'. The outcome is one team aligned for success. The outcome is all Forest Holidays build programmes are under budget, on time and with improved quality.

Our culture, the magic behind our success can be brought down to 5 points which are outlined below:-

1. Leadership
2. Support
3. Attitude
4. Soul
5. Have Fun.

1. Leadership

Our overall 'big picture' strategy is about sustaining our great levels of performance whilst rolling out future sites as we plan for the next stage in the Forest Holidays' life cycle. In order to achieve this strategy we set about focussing on our operating priorities; the four Cs and everyone's objectives fall within these categories and we think they are right for a customer focussing company; Customer, Culture, Cost and Commercial.

It is critical that the business recruits leaders that "walk their talk" and they recruit team players who are of great quality and share the same company culture and values

Creating a fun, lively, high performance environment is also important where people want to work but know they will need to raise their game.

Don't rest on laurels and think you know everything. Particularly the higher up you go in management, always look to learn new things to progress self and company.

Richard Palmer, Forest Holidays Development Director, reminds us of great examples of leadership:

- Get out on site: 'boots on the ground', Leading from the front when in the early days we were having challenges with cleaning cabins – Richard and his wife, Sue over a bank holiday weekend turned up at a site and cleaned cabins themselves from early in the morning until late at night.

- The Freedom to Succeed: Richard often gives his team the 'freedom to succeed' and will always work hard to give his team ALL the credit for the success of the build programme – always looking to give credit to others.

Forest Holidays has engaged a series of Executive Coaches to help support and focus team members to gain support for high performance, and this is really important if you are aiming for a world class company.

Gary Fletcher, CEO at Forest Holidays found John Brown, Forest Holidays Executive Coach, helpful to develop himself and the company's leaders. Latterly, Dan Sullivan at Strategic Coach, and his programme has been such a help to organise and structure the business. Gary is truly indebted to both individuals for their help in developing Forest Holidays and for supporting the incredible journey.

2. Support

The Support Centre is the name of our headquarters, as it describes exactly what it is, supporting the business and front line teams to deliver outstanding service, particularly the non-customer facing departments; IT, Finance, Development, here to service and support Operations, Sales & Marketing and Site Teams to provide great service. Examples below.

- Ross Faith, Forest Holidays Finance Director knows and his team know that if you don't pay a plumber on time, he doesn't turn up when the General Manager on site has a problem. Customers suffer when the heating doesn't work.

- IT – If our booking system isn't working our site teams cannot rebook customers for further stays on site.

- Development has customer impact plans and communicates constantly with our site teams in order to minimise the impact to our customers as they work on sites.

No silos – keep all teams working together and respecting each other's challenges.

Create an open plan office and ensure the senior team also sits within it. No big chairs and exclusive private offices with drink cabinets! 'We're all in this together.'

Invite site teams to the Support Centre so they understand how the Support Centre works.

3. Attitude

Recruit for attitude and train for skill. This maxim is synonymous with Forest Holidays and we have recruited some outstanding candidates:

This translates into:

"I joined because of the culture; trust, respect and it gives me freedom to deliver."
Jill Grinsted, Sales & Marketing Director

"The young company gives me progression and the ability to progress quickly, I was an administrator, then Reservations Manager, then Retail Manager at 2 sites and I'm now aiming for a General Manager position."
Wendy Bosworth, Retail Manager, Blackwood then Sherwood Forest

"I came in to the business as a part time Reservations Agent, progressed to Accounts Clerk, and now I'm the Purchase Ledger Supervisor. I was awarded the Support Centre Team Member of the Year in 2012."
Kat Hart, Purchase Ledger Supervisor

The process for recruitment is to ascertain quickly, early on, if the candidate has the personality to be customer orientated. This sounds easy but Forest Holidays uses several varied methods pending level of appointment, an in-house questionnaire, external personality profiling and combining structured and unstructured meetings and socials, prior to appointment.

We want to set the new team member up for success. They have an induction, on the job training and a 90 day plan and get support from across the team and senior management.

4. Company Soul!

Corporate and Social Responsibility (CSR), as it is called in the corporate world. Team members want to do the right thing for customers and the business, but what really gets team member involvement is the 'Give Back' strategies for the wider good of the community.

Go local strategies

- Forest Holidays' whole ethos is 'go-local'. The experience we want customers to receive is to explore the local community and spend in the local villages and towns.. This means stocking local produce in our Retreats, joint ventures with local attractions and, activity providers. such as canoeing or rock climbing. We make sure they've got the right standard of course but putting that money back into a local economy. Each Forest Holidays site generates around £2m into the local economy each year. Employment has been analysed with both direct employment on site to include management, Support Crew and Cabin Crew (cleaning teams). This culminates in approximately 90 full time equivalent people within a 20-30 mile radius..Nationally this equates to over 700 full time equivalents across the 9 sites.

Sites and Cabin Design

- Green Developed Cabins don't damage woodlands. They often enhance the longevity of the region with green strategies.
- The Forestry Commission is fully engaged with the design and development of the product and the environment the cabin sits within.
- Sites are identified early with the Forestry Commission and the site is designed around the existing forest, so minimal tree removal is necessary.
  Cabins are exclusively designed to sit in a forest location, to sit comfortably in their habitat and to be environmentally focused.

Give Back

- Forest Holidays supports on a national basis the Woodland Trust as it has an ongoing programme to replant trees and is engaged with the key locations the business's brand supports

- Forest Holidays' key focus and priorities are on local communities and projects, either at the Support Centre or across all our cabin sites in the UK. This can be donations in time, money or resources. Examples are raffle prizes, local fetes, quiz nights and on site collections and events to drive support.
- Forest Holidays favours charities in which team members are personally involved, and where they can make a difference in local communities within the UK.

5. Have Fun!

According to C. Zabocki a US psychologist, laughter can not only improve our psychological well-being but also our physical faculties too. It helps reduce pain and improves our sense of well being

We spend 40% of our waking life at work. If we do not enjoy work it can have a big impact on other parts too so it is important to have fun, laugh along the way.

At Forest Holidays we try to have fun as often as possible, enjoying humour in situations and laughing at ourselves. There are many ad hoc social occasions within departments and the whole company has 2 celebrations per year, plus a celebration at Christmas. It pays (within HMRC limits!) for the team to get together, stay over somewhere and let their hair down, and it's great to see people enjoying themselves.

Forest Holidays' *real* meetings take place in the bar! Also for senior managers, a key part of the selection criteria is a 'beer test'.

If there is one person that has been the 'heartbeat' of Forest Holidays and is the organiser of Fun & Culture it is Jo Butler; who has been in charge of payroll, new inductions, health & safety, administration manager, social & travel organiser, etc. from 2006 and above all was responsible for managing the CEO!! All of Forest Holidays recognise the valuable role Jo plays across the company.

The Proof Is in the Pudding...

If we step back and look at where we were just 8 short years ago, we've been on a truly amazing journey. Forest Holidays metrics have been literally transformed. As these charts show, the company has not only increased revenue dramatically, but the service levels have made phenomenal improvement.

	Nights booked	Occupancy	Total Income	Income p/cabin	Sites*	Complaints
2006	16k	40%AYR	£1.2m	1 x	3- 159	15%
2014	186k	90%AYR	£26m	8 x	9 -584	1%

Key Trends	2008	2009	2010	2011	2012	2013
Overall experience	94.8	96.5	95.9	95.3	94.1	94.9
NPS Score	73.4	79.9	74.1	79.0	64.2	73.5
Value for money	n/a	n/a	n/a	87.2	85.1	87.5
Revisit	n/a	n/a	n/a	58.1	56.4	59.4

* Number of sites and cabins

Net Promoter Scores (NPS ™) *

Forest Holidays' Net Promoter Scores 2008-2014

* Net Promoter is an international single score that denotes customer loyalty. Forest Holidays uses external company CSN to call its customers following their stay on a range of customer satisfaction questions, including Net Promoter questions. According to CSN leading companies score between 50-70%.

On average it is recorded by Satmetix that Net Promoter industry leaders out perform their competitors by 2.6 times.

NPS ™ Stars by Industry: UK (CSN data)

Industry	NPS
Forest Holidays (2014 to date)	**77.4**
Mobile Phone/Smartphone handset	69
Banking	62
Computer Hardware	59
Mobile Phone Services	47
Travel Websites	29
Health Insurance	29
Auto Insurance	20
Internet Service	16

*For publication purposes leading brand names have been withdrawn.

Why the Future Looks Bright...

- Firstly we have currently developed 9 sites in Great Britain and the research we have had done by external company indicates there are many more sites that can be developed.

- The appetite from Forest Holidays customers for new sites is incredible; every time we open a new site we are over 90% occupied all through the year. It is industry standard for a new site to take 3 years to build up its customer base; Forest Holidays has instant success.

- The Forest Holidays Departments are in great shape with great leaders to drive the business forward; we have sales & marketing, Operations, IT & Finance & Development which include getting new sites planning permission and building the cabins. All these have great people and systems ready to cope with developing several new sites per year

- Forest Holidays currently has many new sites in the pipeline at various stages and these will come forward over the next few years. A great supply of new sites.

- And then overseas? What about developing Forest Holidays sites across Europe and beyond. This is probably a few years away but is a possibility at some stage.

2 big commercial drivers that make Forest Holidays a winner can be found in other countries too:-

   a. The trends for people to have busy lives and not spend enough time with their partners, families particularly in urban locations. Escape to a beautiful Forest Holiday and relax, spend quality time with partner, family and friends in a quality Eco (Environmentally friendly) cabin in a healthy environment where you can walk, cycle , canoe., rock climb, learn about wildlife, plants & forests.

   b. There are many overseas governments that own forest land and there might be an opportunity to structure a joint venture like the British Forestry Commission with Forest Holidays. Forest Holidays provides a positive cabin rental revenue stream to the Forestry Commission. They have a shareholding in the company and have integrated management across all areas of the business.

Here's How to Learn More about

The Forestry Commission...

www.forestry.gov.uk
www.scotland.forestry.gov.uk
www.naturalresourceswales.gov.uk

Here's How to Learn More about Forest Holidays...

If you would like any further information on Forest Holidays or our business strategies, you can contact us at: www.forestholidays.co.uk. You can follow us at:

Twitter: @forestholidays
Facebook: forest holidays
Pinterest: forest holidays

Here's How to Learn More About Forest Holidays...

Have you ever wondered what sets one company apart from the pack? Why some companies thrive and are fantastic places to work, while at others, you feel like your opinion doesn't matter and you stare at the clock waiting until home time?

Forest Holidays was one such company, where morale couldn't be lower, the future was dim and even the clients were unhappy. Fast forward eight years to today, and in terms of service Forest Holidays is in the top 10% of all companies worldwide. Customers are now raving fans and business is booming. What was the reason for such an abrupt turn-around? Join us as we take you through the reasons behind Forest Holidays journey from ordinary to extraordinary.

Here are three ways you can engage with Forest Holidays right now...

Option 1: Join us in an enchanting location for your very own forest holiday where the simpler luxuries matter more. Visit: www.forestholidays.co.uk to see our world class cabins and reserve your spot today.

Option 2: Follow us on social media and be the first to find out where new locations are being opened all over the UK. You can find us on Facebook, Pinterest and Twitter @forestholidays.

Option 3: If you are passionate about providing outstanding customer service and love the outdoors, and would like the chance to have the freedom to achieve for yourself, apply for a team member position at: http://www.forestholidayscareers.co.uk/

If you have questions, we'd love to help. Send an email to info@ForestHolidays.co.uk and we will get back to you straight way.

About the Author

Gary Fletcher, Chief Executive, Forest Holidays

Born in Staffordshire in the UK, Gary has a wide and varied background, ranging from sports and leisure, property development, franchising and UK tourism.

Gary's early ambition was to become a professional footballer. Indeed he credits his innate understanding of the power of team work, and turning disappointment into success with these early ambitions.

After gaining a sports degree in 1986 he decided to widen his experience working his way around the world undertaking many and varied grounded roles; from bar work, coaching sports, office removals, painting and decorating, porter at a fruit and vegetable market, as well as playing semi pro soccer across a range of UK Clubs, and in Australia, he also coached Ipswich Town youngsters under the legendary Sir Bobby Robson.

His varied work experience and being able to understand the power of team work, and how a business works from all points of view, equipped him well to transform many leisure & tourism businesses performance, to build his own property company and to develop Forest Holidays from small beginnings in 2004 to the successful holiday brand it has become today under his leadership.

Gary lives in Staffordshire with his wife Claire and 3 daughters; Sammie, Ellie and Hanna, and is a passionate Derby County Football Club supporter.

A Massive Thanks to the Team...

A massive personal thank you to all Forest Holidays team members past and present for their valuable contribution to the success of the business so far. I have a few skills but nowhere near what we have as a team. I want to give an unbelievable thank you for an unbelievable journey. I've had such fun. We've had challenges and successes, it's been a great journey and it's all due to the people I get to work with each and every day.

Our team never ceases to amaze me. They always come up with the answers. I'm staggered, absolutely staggered sometimes. In fact, there's another book that the development team should write. How do they build on time, under budget and with increased quality every time? Or maybe the Sales & Marketing Team; how to market a growing business and deliver the staggering occupancy every year? It's just quite astounding what people can do given a bit of freedom to achieve, given the support and focus.

See the list of individuals and companies that have contributed to this great company...

Note: Thanks to Peter Phillipson, Chairman of Forest Holidays for the Title of the book; *Freedom To Achieve*.

HARRY ACKERS	STEFAN BINGHAM
LUCIA ADAMOVA	JAMES BLACK
ROGER ADAMS	JOHN BLUNDELL
LINDA ADCOCK	SARAH BOON
LAURENT AGOSTINELLI	WENDY BOSWORTH
SUE ALBRICE	DEBRA BOWERMAN
GRANT ALLEN	DAVID BOWERMAN
STEPHANIE ALLEN	ROSSALIN BOWGEN
JOHN ALLEN	JEZ BOWKETT
GARETH ALLEN	EMMA BRADIE
ANDREW ALLSOPP	LEE BRASENELL
GEMMA ARMES	NICOLE BRASHIER
SAMUEL ASBURY	EDWARD BRIDESON OATES
LUKE AYERS	WALDO BRITZ
RYAN AYMS	ANDREW BROOK
HELEN BACON	CHRIS BROOKS
THOMAS BACON	KATIE BROTHERS
RITCHIE BADLAND	RONALD BROWN
MARTIN BALLARD	AARON BROWN
MARK BARKER	ANTHONY BROWN
VANESSA BARNES	SELWYN BROWN
JULIE BARNETT	ALAN BURKE
RACHEL BARRELL	CAROLE BURKENSHAW
PHILLIP BARRELL	ADRIAN BURN
SHANE BARTON	AMIE BURNETT
MIKE BASTIMAN	JOANNE BUTLER
EMILY BATCHELOR	NEIL CAMERON
FREYA BATCHELOR	MARK CAMPBELL
CARLY BEDFORD	JENNIFER CARROLL
NICHOLAS BELL	ALAN CHALMERS
JULIETTE BELL	CLAIRE CLACK
STEPHEN BELTON	KATE CLAMP
DAVID BELTON	JAMES CLARKE
DAVID BENNETT	AMANDA CLARKE
FRANKIE BENNETT	KERRY-LOUISE COLEMAN
ANTONIO BETES	MALCOLM CONIFEY
AMANDA BEVERLEY	SHARON CORNEY
ZOWIE BIDEWELL	JOHN COUGHLAN
MARTYN BINGHAM	LAURIE COX

RICHARD CRAWSHAW	ANDREW FRIEDRICH
ANGELA CUMBERPATCH	PAUL FURLEPA
MANUELA DA FONTE	PAT GARLAND
ANDREW DACK	JOHN GARLAND
JOHN DARRELL	JEAN LUIS GELEZ
REBECCA DAVIDSON	JOSH GLYNN
JANICE DAVIES	YVONNE GORDON
DAWN DAVIES	JULIE GOULD
JAMES DAVIS	ALISTAIR GRAHAM
ELLEN DEANS	JOSEPHINE GRANGER
RACHAEL DENNEY	TOMMY GRANGER
LEANNE DIXON	LAURA GRANT
VANESSA DOMINGOS DOS SANTOS	AMANDA GRAY
	STUART GREEN
ANTONY DORLING	KEVIN GREEN
ANGELA DOS SANTOS	ERIC GREEN
MARINA DOSELL	AJ GRIFFIN
THOMAS DOY	JILL GRINSTED
ANGELA DRING	JESSICA GRUDGINGS
DESMOND DRURY	ALAN HARRIS
ANNA DUNKLEY	RICHARD HARRIS
IAN DYSON	KATHRYN HART
PAT DYSON	DANIELLE HART
MIKE EDENS	TALITHA HATCHER
REBECCA ELGAR	PHILIP HAWKINS
SARAH ELPHICK	SARAH HAWKINS
CHARMAINE EMMS	HELEN HEAL
JESSICA ETTERIDGE	TASALA-BELLE HEATH
DALE ETTERIDGE	MARTIN HEATLIE
ROSS FAITH	BLANCHE HEBSON
STUART FANSHAW	EMMA HENN
SILVA FERREIRA	RACHEL HESSOM
JOANNA FINCHEN	KAYLEIGH HIGGINSON
GARY FLETCHER	KYM HIGGS
AMANDA FORDE	BARBARA HILLIER
LAURA-MAI FORDE	CONNOR HOARE
GEMMA FOSTER	MICHAEL HOLLAND
ANDY FOWKES	JOANNE HOLLOWAY
CRAIG FRASER	SIMON HOLT

SALLY HONCHARENKO
KELLY-MARIE HOPE
LINDA HORNBY
CHARLOTTE HOULDER
AMY HOUSEGO
ASHLEY HOWARD
TORI HOWELLS
PAUL HOWES
MACAULEY HUBBARD
SHIFA HUBBARD
ADAM HUNT
CAROLINE HUNT
BEN HURST
JOHN JACQUES
RICHARD JEE
MICHAEL JEFFERSON
KEIRAN JENKINS
TAMARA JENKINS
ANN JEWSBURY
KARL JONES
MILLIE JONES
MATTHEW JONES
HARPEET KAUR
EMMA KEMBLE
JUDITH KERSHAW
LINDA KERSHAW
ROBERT KETT
ALICE KING
KATHERINE KING
JAMES KIRKHAM
LIANE KNAPTON
KAREN KOSLOWSKI
VALERIE LANG
KAREN LANGLEY
SAMANTHA LAWN
IAN LAWRENCE
HAYLEY LAWSON
STEPHANIE LEE
CHRISTINE LEE

TERESA LEVINGBIRD
REBECCA LEWIS
CHRISTOPHER LEYBOURN
EMMA LEYSHON
PAUL ROSS LOCKE
SUZANNE LOVE
MONICA LUCAS
ROBERT MACKIE
ANDREW MACLEOD
JOHN MAGUIRE
AHMED MALEK
NATHAN MALLABY
TANYA MARSHALL
JULIE MCBAIN
NICOLA MCCALL
CALUM MCCRAE
CHRISTINE MCCULLOCH
LUCY MCKAY
IAIN MCMULLAN
DANIEL MEARS
HANNAH MEEK
VICTORIA MELHUISH
MARGARET MENZIES
CHRISTOPHER MILES
BRIAN MITCHARD
DEBBIE MITCHELL
CAROLINE MOIR
HAZEL MOIR
STUART MOIR
ADELAIDE MOREIRA DE OLIVEIRA
JENNIFER MORRIS
GAVIN MORRISON
JAMES MOSS
JAMES MOULINIE
LAUREN MURPHY

JUSTIN NEEDHAM	KATIE ROBINSON
GAIL NEWTON	LYNDA ROBINSON
TIM NIXON	ANDREW ROGERS
KEN NORRIS	CRAIG ROPER
CARRIE OAKES	ANDY RYANS
CHARMAINE OLDKNOW	JULIE SAMPSON
ERIC OWEN	PENNY SCHOFIELD
KAREN OWEN	JONATHAN SCOTT
GAVIN OWEN	JURATE SENDZIKIENE
RICHARD PALMER	CHRISTOPHER SHARKEY
JENNIFER PANTER	NICOLA SHARKEY
MANDY PARIS	EMMA SHAW
DANIEL PARISH	MARK SHEPPARD
REBEKAH PARKER	ANNA SIDWELL
THOMAS PARTINGTON	KATE SKETCHLEY
DOLORES PATALIDIS	STEPHEN SKIDMORE
SCOTT PATTERSON	DALE SKIP
LAURA PEARSON	CHRISTOPHER SMILLIE
ANDREA PEATTIE	CARRON SMITH
SANDRA PENDER	LLOYD SMITH
JESSICA PERRY-QUICK	VICKI SOUTH
SAMANTHA PETRIE	SHAUN SPIERS
PETER PHILLIPSON	JAMIE SPRAKE
EWA POLAK	SPENCER SQUIRES
HENRYK POLAK	GAIL STAPLES
JACOB PRICE	JACK STOCKDALE
ANNE PRINCE	COLIN STOKER
DARREN PRINGLE	MARTIN SUMMERS
EMMA-JANE PROBERT	THOMAS SUNDERLAND
CARON PULLUM	KARL SUNLEY
MARIE QUADLING	KAREN TAIT
JONATHON RAMSAY	AMARJIT TATLA
DAVID READ	DAVID TAYLOR
KEITH RENFREE	LESLEY TAYLOR
ELIZABETH REYNOLDS	SCOTT THOMAS
KATHLEEN RICHES	CARMEN THOMPSON
ZAC RILEY	PAUL THOMPSON
LISA ROBERTS	MICHAEL THORP
	KIMBERLEY TORRANCE

FRANCIS TRIGGLE
ADAM TRUELOVE
JACK TURNER
SCOTT VAUGHAN
CHLOE VILUMS
JOHN WADLEY
HAYDN WARD
ASHLEY WARDLE
DAVID WELSFORD
JAMIE WENMAN
ANTON WESSELS
DAVD WHITECROSS
CHRISTOPHER WHITTINGHAM
RICHARD WHITWELL
STEVEN WILLEMSEN
RAYCHEL WILLIAMS
DERRY WILLIAMS
SARAH WILLIAMS
TERRY WILLIAMSON
ANDREW WILLISON
JULIA WINTERBURN
KELLY WOOD
ANN WOODS
HANNAH WORGAN
CHARLOTTE YATES

Alan Wood Consulting
2 Can
4 Site Surveys
A B Gee of Ripley
A&J Bartlett
AB Internet
ACF Cleaning
AECOM
AJ Outdoors
Alan Motion Tree Consulting
Alan Wood & Partners
Alger Electrics and Alarms
All Points Electrical Services
Alliance
Alrewas Cars
Ampersand Associates
Andrew Davy Electrical
Andrew Westwood
Andy Grove
Andy Lawton Smith
Andy Thornton
Anthony James Insurance
AON UK
Applewood
Approved Design Consultancy
Archaeological Project Services
Aroma Cleaning
Arthur
Ashbon Services
Aspin Foundations
Aspin Foundations
Avery Decorators
Awash Laundry
B&B Innovations
Baca Workwear & Safety
Badgemaster
Baker Ross
Banners Gate Transportation
BC Softwear
Belfield Furnishings
Berry Hill News
BESP Oak Furniture
Bill Pegram
Birdhouse Design
Bishta
Blue Bone Imports Company
Blue Sky
Bob Hill
Bob Macintosh
BOC
Bon Bons
Border Scaffolding Services
Box It Joinery Services
Breadsall priory
Breckland council
Brian Bell Carpets
Brian Lane Joinery
British Gas
BT
Bullivants
Bunzl
Burn Marketing
Burn UK
Caliper
Caliper UK
Calor Gas
Carford Group
Carter Cabin Hire
Carter Flooring
Catalyst Corporate finance
Catalyst Marketing
CBL Leisure Solutions
Cetus Solutions
Champneys
Charlesworth Tree Surgery
Charlie Troman

Cherry Health and Beauty
Chocolati
Chubb Fire
Clarke Banks Limited
Cleaning and Paper Disposables PLC
Click squared
Cloke Associates
CMK Plant Hire
Collins Environmental Consultancy
Coloured Cob Trekking Centre
Concept Town Planning
Conkers
Coopers of Pickering
cornish Orchards
Cottage Delight
Country Choice
Cowal Marketing Group
Cricketts Inn
Cromartie
Cruise Loch Lomond
Crystal Radio Systems
Customer service network
D&D Dairies
D.A.D
Dale Leisure Supplies
Dales Water Services
Dan sullivan
Dapper Doggy's
David Evans Artist
David Hunter
David Welsford
Davies Surveys Limited
DBA
Deloittes
Derby county
Derby Sign and Graphics

Derrick Watson
Dex's Midnight Runners
Directorbank
Dream Copywriting
Duplex Cleaning Machines (UK)
Durham City Interiors
E & A recruitment
EDF Energy
Edmond Shipway
Efi Zazo
Electric Center
English Tree Care
EON Energy Services
Equanet
Ernst & young
Espares
Evans Property Group
Farmer neil
Filter4spa
Fire Protection Group
Firebelly Stoves
First Choice Coffee
First Hand Productions
Flaco UK
Flights of Fancy
Flogas Britain
Forest of Dean Adventure Tower and Topes
Forestry Commission
Forestry Commission Scotland
Fourth
Fox Print
Franchise development Centre
Frank Haighton Forestry
Freeth Cartwrights
FRK Groundworks

FST group
FST Marketing Communications
G.Vasey
Gailarde
Garry Barr
GIA
GIA Architects
Glass Solutions
Go Ape
Google Ireland
Grant Thornton
Green Square Renewable Energy
Green Tourism Business Scheme
Greenhatch Group
Greenlife Renewables
H.A.T Mechanical Engineers
H20 Linen Services
Halls Roofing
Hands on 2012
Harp Wallen
Haven Power
Hawthornes Timber
HB Graphics
Hearing Dogs for Deaf People
Heart of the National Forest
Hentland Group
Heyland and Whittle
High Speed Training
High Voltage Systems and Services
High Water (Scotland)
Hitchenor wakeford
Holder Mathias Architects Plc
Hoseasons Group
House of Marbles
Howard CC Gosling

HR Solutions
Huggabubba
Humberside Wrappings
Humberts
Hydraguard
Ian Hobbs
Ian Williams
ICI Paint
Igxglobal UK
Indigo Art
Infinium Associates
Inspired Scaffolding Services
International Visual
Intuitus Limited
JAA Media
Jamie's Italian
Jeremy Millington
Jewsons
JLA
John Anderson
John Ayling and Associates
john brown
john lillie
John Webster
Jones Lang Lasalle
JQ Contracts
Karl Schorman
Karndean
Keith Carter Plastering
Keycraft
Kingfisher Environmental Services
Konstructa Hire
Koris
KPMG
LA Hall (Hull)
Lauden Chocolate
Laverstoke Park Farm
Legends of Nottingham

- Leisure Concepts
- len Worrell
- Lloyds Bank
- Lloyds Development Capital
- Locatel UK
- Loch Lomond & Trossachs National Park
- Loch Lomond Brewery
- Lockhart Catering Equipment
- Locktite Security Services
- Love Loch Lomond
- LWC Central
- Lynn Webster Consultants
- Lyreco
- Mad About Pies
- Magnet
- Managed Waste Solutions
- Martin Draper
- Martin Kingston
- Martineau
- Mastercraft Rugs
- Mel Wombwell
- Menu Shop
- MG Leisure Developments
- michael Paul
- Mico Lighting
- mike Ballantyne
- Mischon de Reya
- Mitie Pest Control
- Mitre
- Monica Lucas
- Morley Hayes
- Mr Pitchfork's Pickles
- MSQ Interiors
- My Personal Sanctuary
- Nationwide Hygiene Supplies
- Natural Resources Wales
- Neil Sanderson
- Nick Hart
- Nigel Edwards
- no5 Chambers
- Npower Business
- Office Depot
- Ogilvie
- Omobono
- Online Systems
- Oobstock
- Overton Black Arrows
- Paige Solutions
- Palmer and Harvey mclane
- Panks Engineers
- Partnerships UK
- Paul Isaacs
- PCS Technology
- Peter Phillipson
- Peter Price
- Peter Weiss
- Peter Wilcock
- Phil Rank
- Pinelog
- Pinsent Masons
- PJ Mastics
- Planning Solutions Consulting
- PLQ Pellets
- Poppies Hotel
- Prelude Consulting
- Presige Park and Leisure Homes
- Pricewaterhouse Coopers LLP
- Propellernet
- PSC
- Pukka Herbs
- Purely Cornish
- Quibell
- R&M Scaffolding

R&S Robertson
RA Dalton
Rachel & Sam Dalton Thorpe
Rackspace
Raleigh UK
RD health & safety
RE Marshall
Regent Digital Document Solutions
Results International
Retail Systems Technology
Richard Matthews
Richard Smith
Right Directions
RM Refrigeration & Air Conditioning
Robert Louden
Roger Bullivant
Roger Vail
Ropservices UK
Russells (Kirbymoorside)
Ryedale Skip Hire
Sabina Voysey
Sage Pay
Savills
Scarborough Decorators
Scarborough Spas
Scott Thompson
Screwfix Direct
senn consulting
Seton
Signs Workshop
Silver Travel Advisor
Sinclair Heating
SJB
Sky Business
Specflue
Springhead Brewery
SRP Risk and Finance LLP
Stephen Macluskie
Steve Biggins
Steve Brown
Steve Duckworth
Steve Westbrook
Strategic coach
Stuart Roberts
Tartan Timber
Taylor lane
Taylor Made Adventures
Taylors of Harrogate
Taylors of Pickering
TBS
Tealeaf
The Cook Kitchen
The Cornish Curry Company
The Franchising Centre
The Great Big Tree Climbing Co
The Great Yorkshire Brewery PPL
The Jubilee Inn
The Kitchen Equipment Company
The New Inn and Cropton Brewery
The Play Inspection Company
The Purple Olive
Thomas Allan & Sons
Thorpe Woodlands Adventure Centre
Tiger Scaffolding
Tiger TIM Products
TK Refrigeration
Toby Charlwood
Toby Laparge Norris
Tods Murray LLP
Total Licensing Solutions

Tractor Hire
Travers Smith LLP
Tree Maintenance Limited
TV Net
Tweddell and Slater
Twitter International Company
UK Electrical Services
Unlimited Events
Uplands Construction
Verifone Services UK and Ireland
Victoria Edwards
Visit Cornwall
Visit England
Visit Loch Lomond
Visit Norfolk
Visit Scotland
Visit York
Vodafone
Voyager PR
Warren Rumsey
Water Treatment Products
Welcome to Yorkshire
West Sussex Archaeology
William Allen
Wissenbach
Wolseley UK
woodberry
Woodland Trust Charity
Wragge Lawrence Graham and Co LLP
Wybone
Wyedean Canoe and Adventure Centre

www.ingramcontent.com/pod-product-compliance
Lightning Source LLC
Chambersburg PA
CBHW071817170526
45167CB00003B/1343